This book provides a brief and straight-forward introduction to the Gaelic language. Keeping things as simple as possible, George McLennan's aim is to explain the *why* of Gaelic expression.

Readers who may be taking a first look at the language are accommodated, and those whose knowledge of Gaelic is a little more advanced have also found the book useful.

Since the first edition in 1983, the potential benefits of bilingualism have become more generally understood. In this new updated edition **Scots Gaelic – a brief introduction** will continue to be a valuable basic guide to the Gaelic language.

George McLennan is an author and scholar of language. He lives in Argyll.

Scots Gaelic

a brief introduction

George McLennan

Argyll
publishing

© George McLennan

First published 1987
Gairm Publications
Glasgow

This edition 1998
Argyll Publishing
Glendaruel
Argyll PA22 3AE

**Chuidich Comhairle nan Leabhraichean
am foillsichear le cosgaisean an leabhair seo.**

**British Library Cataloguing-in-Publication Data.
A catalogue record for this book is available
from the British Library.**

ISBN 1 874640 19 X

Origination
Cordfall Ltd, Glasgow

Printing
Caledonian International
Book Manufacturing, Glasgow

To Dorothy

Contents

Preface

The continuing expansion of interest in Gaelic has led to a demand for a new edition of *Scots Gaelic – a brief introduction*. I have therefore taken this opportunity to expand some of the points made earlier and to give additional illustrations, all of which I hope will make the book more useful.

Now that the potential benefits of bilingualism are fully understood, it is clear that a knowledge of Gaelic as well as English – and/or any other language(s) – is a considerable asset, not, as was sometimes thought, a drawback. In addition, continuing European integration should encourage us to view Gaelic in a European dimension, beyond the traditional Celtic fringe.

George McLennan
Blairmore, Argyll
January 1998

Preface

to the first edition

Until quite recently the study of Gaelic has been greatly neglected, even discouraged, in this country. Many Scots who are familiar with other European languages often know little or nothing about Gaelic, and seem to regard it as being somehow outwith the mainstream of European languages.

The purpose of this booklet, then, is to provide a brief introduction to the Gaelic language with a selective discussion of its main features. I have tried to keep things as simple as possible to accommodate readers who may be taking a first look at the language, but those whose knowledge of Gaelic is a little more advanced may also find the booklet useful.

Accordingly, while a lot more could be said on many points, and qualifications added here and there, I have preferred to be brief rather than punctilious. Thus, guides to pronunciation, for instance, are inevitably only approximate. Readers should also be aware that Gaelic orthography is not as uniform as that of English, although steps continue to be taken towards an agreed standard. For example, the new system of accentuation (using mainly the grave accent) is used, but a note in chapter 5 describes the older system, in use until very recently in printed books.

In contrast to native speakers, who absorb the language as children, adults who are learning Gaelic from scratch often derive much benefit from knowing *why* the language takes shape as it does. I have tried to bear this in mind throughout the booklet.

1

Background

SCOTS GAELIC belongs to the Celtic branch of the Indo-European family of languages. The other Celtic languages are Irish and Manx (Isle of Man) which, with Gaelic, have a common ancestor called Gadelic; and Welsh, Breton (Brittany, France) and Cornish, whose common ancestor is Brittonic. Today Gaelic, Irish, Welsh, Breton and – only just – Manx survive as modern examples of the Celtic language which was spoken in many parts of Western Europe as far east as the Danube up to the time of the Roman Empire. It was the Romans who destroyed the Celtic languages in mainland Europe, and in their place we find today the Romance languages (Italian, French, Spanish, Portuguese, Romanian etc) all derived from Latin. Thus the Breton language in France is not indigenous, but was taken there by settlers from Cornwall and Wales around the fifth century AD. Scots Gaelic itself came from Ireland at about the same time, and for many centuries Gaelic and Irish were very similar, at least on a literary level (small though this was).

The point about the Indo-European family of languages, of which Celtic is one branch, is that most of the European languages of today (over thirty of them) go back to a common ancestor called Indo-European. Consequently, we can expect many Gaelic words to be related to, or cognate with, words in other European languages. On a more local level, Gaelic vocabulary obviously has many similarities with Irish, Welsh, etc; but many learners of Gaelic are unfamiliar with these languages, and so throughout this booklet a selection of Gaelic words is given with cognates in English.*

There are, of course, a large number of words in Gaelic which are simply taken from English, sometimes altered a little and spelt in the Gaelic way: eg **adag** for "haddock", **banca** for "bank" and so on. As a general rule they represent things outside the traditional Gaelic environment, such as words for "factory", "hospital" etc. and the machines found in them. This is especially true of modern scientific terms – television, car, rocket etc. In many cases Gaelic words have in fact been created for such words – **x-ghath** for "x-ray", for instance – but most native speakers use the English word. Often they would not be familiar with the newly created Gaelic word, so that if one hears eg **saideal** for "satellite" on the radio, it is usually accompanied by an English "translation" – at least the first time round – to make it understood. However, efforts in Gaelic broadcasting to strive towards a Gaelic unadulterated by constant intrusions of English are a welcome sign.

This use of English words has, of course, the advantage of making Gaelic easier for a learner to understand, even if the words are in Gaelic dress, eg **depeandadh** for "depending", or **smocadh** for "smoking". In addition to the many English words in Gaelic there are many from Scots, often reflecting Scots pronunciation, eg **gròiseid**, "grosset" (gooseberry), or **saighdear**, "soldier".

However, the vast majority of Gaelic words are, of course, not borrowed from English, though many have cognates with English. Thus **eaglais**, "church", needs only a moment's

*Sometimes, of course, a cognate is more clearly seen in another European language; eg **muileann** (mill) and French "moulin", **caraid** (friend) and Italian "caro", **fhuair** (found) and Greek (Archimedes) "heureka".

thought before one sees the connection with "ecclesiastic". Since it is much easier to learn vocabulary if one can see such connections, a list of words will be given at the end of each chapter, with cognates in English. It is often a question of not seeing the wood for the trees. English is unusual in that it is a language composed of two separate strata – 1, a Germanic one, the basis, and 2, a classical (mainly Latin) one. The latter is a more learned, artificial stratum. It is as if there were two languages within English, either one capable of being translated into the other. Thus "two-yearly" (Germanic) = "biennial" (Classical), "cogitate" (Classical) = "think" (Germanic) and so on.

Generally, of course, good written English combines the two strata although it is often possible to write predominantly in one as opposed to the other. Many Gaelic words, then, are cognate with the learned, classical word in English, as in the case of **eaglais**. Equally, many Gaelic words are cognate with an English word which is slightly removed in meaning from the immediate English translation, although the connection is usually clear enough. Here are some examples:

VOCABULARY

Gaelic	English	English Cognate
aifreann	mass (religious)	offering
bàirneach	limpet	barnacle
cailc	chalk	calcium
dall	blind	dull
each	horse	equine
facal	word	vocal
gailleann	storm	gale
ifrinn	hell	infernal
leabhar	book	library
madainn	morning	matins
nathair	snake	adder (originally nadder)
obair	work	operate

peileir	bullet	pellet
rannsaich	search	ransack
sagart	priest	sacerdotal, sacred
tana	thin	tenuous
uileann	elbow	ulna

2

Aspiration

ASPIRATION, also (and more correctly) called lenition, is one of the chief difficulties for learners of Gaelic. On paper it takes the form of a letter "h" inserted after a consonant and is very frequent in Gaelic (and even more frequent in pseudo-Gaelic). Aspiration, or lenition, is the lightening or softening of a consonant when it occurs between two vowels. In going from one vowel to the other the consonant in between is not made in the normal way, but extra air is allowed through. For instance, the clear, crisp sound of "c" (as in English "cut") becomes, when aspirated, "ch" (as in "loch"). In other words, the tongue in this case does not go all the way through with its usual movement towards the roof of the mouth to produce "c" but stops short, and "ch" results.

In a sense it is a kind of relaxation of pronunciation in that the effort is not made to make the clear consonant sound between vowels, and so the lightened, or lenited consonant results. This does not mean, of course, that there is anything slovenly about it. Every language has its own ways of adapting sounds in various uses and combinations to suit the speakers of that language.

Thus in the English of southern England a final "r" is not pronounced, nor, colloquially, is an initial "h". The famous

Scots glottal stop, where the "t" in, eg "water" is lightened in sound so as to almost disappear, has a resemblance to the lightened consonant in Gaelic. Modern French also provides numerous examples, as "croire" (to believe) from Latin "credere" (whereas Italian "credere" keeps the "d"). Gaelic aspiration, of course, is a well established, and in the correct circumstances, which will be explained later, a quite obligatory feature of the language.

The difficulty for beginners is the different sounds some of the consonants make when aspirated. Here are the aspirated Gaelic consonants with the phonetic English equivalents:

bh = v
ch = ch
dh = gh (with a broad vowel) or y (with a slender vowel).
                                              See chapter 3
fh is silent
gh = gh or y, as with dh above
mh = v
ph = f
sh = h
th = h

It is hard to see why "mh", for instance, should have the sound of "v". In fact the "h" is only a symbol indicating that the consonant is aspirated; at one time a dot above the letter did the same job. The sounds of "ch" (as in "loch") and "ph" (as in "photograph") are more obvious, and so "h" has been used in other cases.

Some of the other letters have interesting parallels in Europe. A modern Greek and Russian B is pronounced V, a modern Greek gamma ("g") followed by a slender vowel is pronounced "y" (as in "yet"). To take an illustration closer to home, "yett" is a Scots variant of "gate". Spanish often does not sound an initial "f" from Latin (eg "hado" – fate – Latin "fatum", Italian "fato" etc); and "p" and "f" are often inter-changeable within the Germanic languages, eg "ship" and German "schiff".

It is when listening to spoken Gaelic that learners find aspiration difficult. A word which begins with, say, "b" will sometimes begin with the sound "v" – and so on with the other consonants. So, words beginning with consonants have two ways of being pronounced initially, depending on the grammatical circumstances. One has to learn two words, as it were. Thus the Gaelic for "cow" is "**bò**" (unaspirated) or "**bhò**" (aspirated) and the sounds are "bo" and "vo" respectively. This feature is found in other European languages, and even in some African languages, but it is above all a phenomenon of the Celtic languages. Scots Gaelic is particularly fond of it, more so than its parent Irish.

When consonants are aspirated in the middle, or at the end, of words they are frequently not sounded at all. Thus **deigh**, "ice" is pronounced "jayi". This is easier to understand as it frequently happens in English, eg "high", "sigh", "throughout". At an earlier stage in the language such consonants were pronounced, both in Gaelic (**Gàidhlig** > Gadelic) and in English, which is why they still appear in the word, though now silent. They may, in fact, still be sounded in a cognate in another language; for instance the "g" is pronounced in German "burg" ("town", Hamburg, Salzburg, etc) but in Scots "burgh" the hard "g" sound has gone. A silent aspirated consonant in English is often sounded elsewhere in Europe - thus Scots and German "licht", but English "light".

Gaelic has gradually been increasing the use of aspirated consonants over the centuries, and, as befits a living language, the process continues today. For instance, **dhomh**, "to me" is now far more common than the rarely heard initially unaspirated **domh**. Sometimes too a final consonant may, or may not, be aspirated depending on the speaker. For instance the adverb **gu h-àraid**, "especially", is given a final "j" sound by some speakers, but there is also an aspirated form **gu h-àraidh**, where the final "dh" is not sounded at all.

Gaelic has at least retained such aspirated consonants in its spelling, even if they are not pronounced, and this can make a word easier to understand. Thus **màthair**, "mother" is pronounced "ma-h-er", but because the "t" is written we can see the obvious connection with "maternal" etc. French "mère", in contrast, also cognate with Latin "mater", has typically lost the "t" from both sound and spelling.

Sometimes an aspirated consonant inside a word may, or may not, be sounded, depending on the speaker. For instance **àbhaist**, "usual", is often heard with the "v" sound in the middle, but many speakers leave it out.

Initial Aspiration

There are, of course, grammatical rules which dictate when the first consonant of a word must be aspirated and they are found in all grammars. Briefly, the main occasions are:

(a) Verbs – to form the past tense eg **cùm**, "keep", **chùm e**, "he kept".
  If the verb begins with a vowel or "f" then it cannot be aspirated in the normal way ; instead, "dh" is put in front of it. This "dh" is connected with the particle **do** which was a sign of the past tense, still found in negatives and questions. Thus **dh'òl mi**, "I drank", **dh'fhàg mi**, "I left".
  Another tense which is aspirated is the subjunctive (= would) eg **chanainn**, "I would say".

(b) Nouns, if they are feminine, aspirate after the definite article singular eg **muir**, "sea", **a' mhuir**, "the sea".*

* The reason for this is that in Gadelic the feminine singular definite article ended in a vowel (as is normal in European languages) and so the

After a preposition with the definite article both masculine and feminine nouns aspirate (although not all consonants do it) eg **air a' bhòrd**, "on the table".

(c) Adjectives, which in Gaelic follow the noun, are aspirated if the noun is feminine eg **tè bheag**, "a small one", "a dram".

(d) A very few adjectives precede their noun, and in this case the noun is aspirated. The most common adjectives to do this are **droch**, "bad", **deagh**, "good", and **ath**, "next". Some other words aspirate nouns which follow them, most notably **mo**, "my", **do**, "your", **a**, "his" and **glè**, "very".

It was noted at the beginning of this chapter that aspiration is the conventional, if unsatisfactory, term for the process subsequently discussed. True aspiration (aka preaspiration), however, ie the insertion of the sound "h", is a feature of Gaelic and is frequently found in short syllables before "c", "p" and "t". Thus **cat**, "cat" is pronounced "caht", **mac**, "son" is pronounced "mahc", and so on. This was a linguistic feature of the old Norse of the Vikings and is a legacy of their stay in the Highlands and Islands.

VOCABULARY

Gaelic	English	English Cognate
ainm	name	onomatopoeia
bata	stick	bat
Callainn	New Year's Day	calendar
diathad, dìot	dinner	diet
eadar	between	international
fear	man	virile
geòla	small boat	yawl

first consonant of the following noun is flanked by two vowels and is therefore aspirated. The masculine definite article ended in a consonant and so there is no aspiration. In the genitive singular, on the other hand, the masculine article did end in a vowel, which is why masculine nouns with the article are aspirated in the genitive singular.

luach	value, worth	lucre
maide	stick	mast
a-nochd	tonight	nocturnal
òraid	speech	oration
pàisd	child (esp. male)	page
rìgh	king	regal
saighead	arrow	Sagittarius
tìr	land	terrain

3

Spelling

GAELIC SPELLING follows clear rules, and is no better or no worse than English in this respect once the rules are understood, and, as a bonus, the sounds produced within the spelling system are a lot more consistent than those of English. But learners of the language, faced with a long Gaelic word half the letters of which do not seem to be pronounced, often do not know where to start! Even native speakers, particularly of the older generation, can often be in difficulties, for several reasons.

Firstly, the shameful attitude of education authorities in the past to Gaelic meant that Gaelic speaking children were, to a large extent, denied an opportunity to be fully literate in their language. Fortunately this attitude has changed greatly in recent years and present trends are very encouraging. Secondly, there has been, until relatively recently, a dearth of reading material in Gaelic, particularly of newspapers and other lighter material. Gaelic books in the past tended to be of a serious, often religious nature, with little suitable for children, for instance. Again, encouraging steps have been taken in recent years to remedy this. Above all, of course, Gaelic has for some centuries been part of an oral culture in which literacy was not essential, and written English was always used when required.

The main feature of Gaelic spelling is the use and influence of the vowels. These are divided into two groups: a) A O U, the broad vowels; and b) E I, the narrow or slender vowels.* Such a division is, of course, common in other European languages, and, as in Gaelic, has an effect on the sound of a consonant next to the vowels. In English, for instance, the letter "c" is pronounced hard (k) with a broad vowel (cat, cot, cut) but soft (s) with a slender vowel (cell, city). This is fairly widespread; compare, eg Italian *Caruso* and *cello*.

The rule in Gaelic spelling is that in a word of more than one syllable, if the last vowel of one syllable is broad, the first vowel of the next syllable must be broad too, eg **seòmar**, "room". Like must be followed by like on either side of the intervening consonant(s). If the last vowel is slender, the first of the next syllable must be slender too, eg **caileag**, "girl". There is a good reason for all this. As we have seen, a broad vowel can give a consonant a different sound from a slender vowel, whether before or after the consonant. Thus the "s" sound (as in English "say") of **cas**, "foot" and **sàil**, "heel", but the "sh" sound (as in English "ship") of **ris**, "to" and **sin**, "that". As a result, it would be confusing if a consonant were to be flanked by a broad vowel on one side and a slender vowel on the other. With a combination of, say . . . **ase** . . . it would not be clear how the "s" was to be pronounced. When the Gaelic spelling rule is followed there is no confusion with this and the other consonants. If there is no consonant between the vowels then the rule obviously doesn't apply – eg **dèan**, "do".

Behind the spelling rule (to which there are a few exceptions, notably past participles) lies ease of pronunciation which has adapted words in such a way that the rule simply reflects the sounds produced by the speakers of the language.

*Compare the vowel order in Ogham (an early form of Gadelic script):

╂	╫	╫	╫	╫
A	O	U	E	I

From the above it is clear that vowels are often found in a word in conformity with the rule and may not have an actual sound of their own. This is one of the reasons why Gaelic words sometimes seem rather long and full of unpronounced letters. Take the word "pibroch" for instance. This is obviously an English spelling, since Gaelic would not allow the slender "i" and the broad "o" to flank the consonants. So the Gaelic spelling is made up as follows: **pìob**, "a pipe"; **pìobair**, "a piper"; **pìobaireachd**, "piping". Twelve letters in Gaelic, seven in English ! Yet the pronunciation of both words is roughly similar – indeed, "pibroch" is intended to be an English phonetic spelling of **pìobaireachd**.

Most consonants have a different sound when they are in conjunction with a broad, or a slender, vowel. The most striking cases are D, L, S, T.

D with a slender vowel is like English "j", eg **Diùra**, "Jura".
D with a broad vowel is closer to English "d", eg **dol**, "going".
L with a slender vowel is like English "li" in "pavilion", eg **leth**, "half".
L with a broad vowel is rather like English "l" in "although", eg **latha**, "day".
S has already been mentioned.
T with a slender vowel is like English "ch", eg **teth**, "hot".
T with a broad vowel is closer to English "t", eg **tarbh**, "bull".

The main point to bear in mind, then, is that different languages, Gaelic included, can use letters of the alphabet in different ways to represent different sounds. For instance, the letter "j" does not have the same sound in German as it does in English. So it is not surprising that Bonnie Prince Charlie's name may not look too familiar in Gaelic, since it cannot begin with the letters "Ch". These two letters in Gaelic give the guttural sound found in "loch"; the required sound, as indicated above, is achieved instead by using the letter "t" with a slender vowel, giving **Teàrlach**.

It has sometimes been suggested that Gaelic would be rather easier to read if it were written phonetically. There have been instances of this in the past, and Manx Gaelic, which is now being successfully revived and is quite close to Scottish Gaelic, is written phonetically. But there are objections. The phonetic scheme suggested is, of course, always English-based, which hardly seems a forward step. But above all, the etymology of the word is destroyed. Consider the word **Di-dòmhnaich**, "Sunday". In this word the aspirated "m" is silent – in no way unusual, as we have seen.* So **dòmhnaich** sounds rather like "dawnich" or "donich". But with the "m" retained in the Gaelic spelling we can see the cognate, Latin "dominus", "lord", "master", Scots "dominie", and thus the word obviously means "the Lord's Day". So correct spellings can be a help in remembering the meaning of a word.

In this connection it is interesting to note that certain products, eg whisky, are now being marketed in Gaelic spelling to give a touch of authenticity, romance, mystery etc. Previously the belief was that calling a product **glè mhath**, "very good" , for instance, might have restricted sales unless it was written in the English phonetic pronunciation Glayva.

Aspiration has been changing the sounds and spellings of Gaelic words for centuries, and while this often hinders the recognition of a Gaelic word when it is spoken – eg **bùth**, "shop", is English "booth", but the "th" is silent in Gaelic** – it is sometimes the English word which is at fault, so to speak.

* The "m" retains its influence, however, by making the preceding "o" nasal. Gaelic makes considerable use of nasal vowels.

** English "th" is not now a used Gaelic sound, although the Hebridean pronunciation of an "r" with slender vowel (another Norse influence) comes near to it.

Thus the pronunciation of English "psalm" with the "l" silent disguises its identity with Gaelic **salm** (pronounced "salam").

In many cases, especially with words borrowed from English, an unpronounced aspirated consonant is inserted simply to separate syllables, or to end a word. For instance, **staidhre** is the Gaelic spelling of English "stair" and **pàigh** the Gaelic spelling of "pay". The aspirated consonants most used in this way are "bh", "dh", "gh", and "th".

VOCABULARY

Gaelic	English	English Cognate
airgead	silver, money	argent
beannachd	blessing,farewell	benediction
cead	permission	cede
dìreach	straight, exact	direct
easbaig	bishop	episcopal
feasgar	evening	vesper
glas	lock	clasp
mair	last, endure	moratorium
òsda	hotel	hostel
pòs	marry	spouse
roth	wheel	rotate
saoghal	world	secular
tràill	slave	thrall

4

Inflection

GAELIC is an inflected language. An inflected language is one in which nouns and adjectives change their form according to whether they are the subject of a sentence, or the object, or some other case. Modern English has largely lost its inflections, but the pronouns "I", "he", "she", "we" and "they" illustrate the point; in Standard English they can be used only when they are the subject. When they are the object we use "me", "him", "her", "us" and "them". In Gaelic it is the nouns and adjectives which change, and this provides a further difficulty for learners.

Living languages are, of course, changing all the time and inflection is a typical feature of them in their earlier stages. Thus Latin is heavily inflected, but most of the modern languages derived from it – eg French, Italian, Spanish and Portuguese – have done away with such changes in the word.*
Some other modern languages which are still inflected, eg Greek, have fewer changes in words than they used to have. Gaelic too has fewer. In its earlier form Gadelic (the ancestor of Gaelic, Irish and Manx) there were five different forms of a noun in the singular, and another five in the plural. Modern Gaelic is much simpler, as we shall see.

* Romanian, however, is still partially inflected.

The main difficulty in Gaelic is the genitive case, which is the "of" form of a word. **Clach**, for instance is "stone"; if we wish to say "of a stone", the form is **cloiche**.* It corresponds, then, to the English possessive case "stone's". Unfortunately for learners there is no single way of forming the genitive in Gaelic; rather, there are several groups of words in which the genitive is formed in the same way. However, the position can be simplified to an extent. The majority of nouns insert an "i" in the genitive, as with **clach**, (quoted above), or, eg **fir**, the genitive of **fear**, "man", and the existing vowel(s) is frequently modified. In origin this "i" is the same as that found in the Latin genitive "domini" (of the lord). In Gadelic too it forms the last letter of the word. In modern Gaelic, however, it has affected the interior of the word. The effect of this, particularly with the letters "d", "t" and "s", is a softening of the otherwise hard final consonant, as explained in the previous chapter. Thus **bàs**, "death" (pronounced baass); **bàis**, "of death" (pronounced baash).

A noun may also have a final "e" in the genitive, as in **cloiche** above, and some nouns have a final "a", eg **gutha**, "of a voice". This again reflects typical Indo-European inflection. Finally, the corollary of the "i" inserted to indicate the genitive is that if a word has an "i" in it already then in many cases the genitive removes that "i", eg **sùil**, "eye", **sùla**, "of an eye".

Adjectives also form their genitive by inserting an "i", with an additional final "e" in feminine cases.

However, the genitive is not as widely used as it used to be, particularly in colloquial Gaelic. For instance, although the genitive of **obair**, "work", is **obrach** (a further class of

*The connection between the two different cases may not always be apparent to beginners. For instance in the place names **An t-Allt Beithe** (Aultbea – the stream of the birch tree) and **Taigh an Uillt** (Taynuilt – the house of the stream) **allt** and **uillt** are the same word, the latter simply being the genitive form, "of the stream".

genitives!) it is not always used in everyday speech. The strict use of many genitives is often felt to be an indication of learned, "correct" speech, formal and educated, a feature of written Gaelic, for example. This falling out of use of many genitives varies according to locality, and to the "standing" and age of the speaker, with the older generation tending to preserve them. Indeed, a word such as **dibhe**, the genitive of **deoch**, "drink" would not only seldom be used colloquially, but would be quite unfamiliar to many younger speakers. All this is perfectly understandable, and, indeed, inevitable. Gaelic is simply following the tendency which has already taken place in other European languages, and continuing its process of simplification. In the case of the genitive this process is assisted by the increasing use of the word **de**, "of" which does away with the need for a separate genitive form.

The other cases are much simpler. The so-called dative case is the name given to the form of the noun used after prepositions – "in", "on", "at", "to" etc. In this case we simply aspirate the first letter of the noun if it is "b", "c", "g", "m" or "p", otherwise there is no change.* Thus **bòrd**, "table", **air a' bhòrd**, "on the table". This applies to both masculine and feminine nouns, except that feminine nouns generally use the aspirated genitive form (minus the final "e"), eg **bròg**, "shoe", **air a' bhròig**, "on the shoe". As we have seen, however, there can be a reluctance to acknowledge an inflected form, so although **clann**, "children", for example, has the genitive form **cloinne**, one is just as likely to hear **leis a' chlann**, "with the children" as the more correct **leis a' chloinn**.

In the vocative case, the form used when someone is addressed directly, the first letter of the noun is again aspirated, eg **a Mhàiri**, "Mairi!" With masculine names the genitive form (the one with an "i" in it) is aspirated, thus **a Sheumais**, "Seumas!"

---

*Unless the word begins with "s" – see next chapter.

There are two main ways of forming the plural in Gaelic:
a) by adding -**an** or -**ean** (spelling rule!) to the singular, eg
làmh, "hand", **làmhan**, "hands"; both masculine and feminine
nouns do this;
b) many masculine nouns have a plural form like the genitive
singular, ie with an inserted "i", eg **each**, "horse", **eich**,
"horses". This is rather like English monosyllables such as
"mouse", "foot", etc. with their plurals "mice", "feet", where a
slender vowel(s) replaces the broad vowel(s) of the singular.
Sometimes both forms of plurals are used with the same
word in different districts; thus **dealbh**, "picture", for instance,
has the plurals **dealbhan** and **deilbh**.

There is also a quite distinct plural which involves the
addition of the ending -**(a)ichean**, eg **litir**, "letter", **litrichean**,
"letters". This form is frequently used in modern words
borrowed from English, so that one hears **busaichean**,
"buses", **loidhnichean**, "lines".

VOCABULARY

Gaelic	English	English Cognate
àirneis	furniture, fittings	harness
beò	living	biology
ceangal	tie, connect	cincture
donn	brown	dun
eile	other	alien
fèileadh	kilt	veil
gobhal	fork	gable
a-màireach	tomorrow	morrow
peacadh	sin	impeccable
prìomh	first	prime
ruadh	red	ruddy
sean	old	senile
taigh	house	tegula, thatch
uisge	water	whisky (water of life)

5

Letters Lost or Added,
Stress and Accent

WE HAVE ALREADY seen how Gaelic pronunciation
sometimes disguises the connection of a word with its English
cognate, and how the similarity is clearer when the word is
written down. In some cases, however, the written form of
the word needs an explanation before we can see the
connection. Gaelic treatment of the letter "p" is an example.
Early Gaelic did not have this "p" sound which was present
in other European languages. Thus the Latin "pater", "father",
takes the form "padre", "père", "paternal" in Italian, French
and English, but the Gaelic form is **athair**. Bearing this loss
of "p" in mind we can see the connection between the following:

GAELIC	ENGLISH	ENGLISH COGNATE
ùr	new, fresh	pure
eun	bird	pen (ie quill)
iasg	fish	piscivorous, Pisces
làn	full	plentiful
leathann	broad	platypus
sir	search	speir (Scots)
uircean	piglet	porcine

Sometimes the "p" is missing inside the word:

teth	hot	tepid
caora	sheep	Capricorn

Sometimes the "p" is replaced by another consonant:

seachd	seven	septet

Present day Gaelic words which begin with "p" are not original, but have been borrowed, mainly from Latin, French and English.

Another factor is metathesis , which refers to consonants changing places within a word, as in the two English forms "girdle" and "griddle". Thus in Gaelic **còisir**, "choir" is from "chorus", **susbaint** from "substance", and **seanailear** from "general" (rank).* Sometimes, in addition to this interchange of consonants there is also a missing "p" to take into account; thus **làmh**, "hand" is cognate with "palm", and **baist** with "baptize".

Yet another factor concerns masculine nouns which begin with a vowel, and feminine nouns (and masculine in some cases) which begin with an "s". Such words have a "t" inserted between themselves and the definite article, eg **an t-ìm**, "the butter", **an t-sràid**, "the street". In the latter instance the "s" is not pronounced. Consider the name Macintyre, which means "son of the joiner, carpenter" (**saor**). The Gaelic form is **Mac an t-Saoir**.

In some cases in Gaelic the "t" has become attached by analogy to a word borrowed from another language; thus **tiota**, "a moment", "a little", is from Greek/Latin "iota", "a

*The form of **seanailear** may also be influenced by the ending **-air** which is used in Gaelic to describe an agent, someone who does something, eg **iasgair**, "fisherman", **clachair**, "mason".

jot". If the foreign word began with an "h" ("h" being mainly a sign of aspiration in Gaelic and not a letter in its own right) then the same thing could happen; thus **talla**, "hall", **taigeis**, "haggis", **togsaid**, "hogshead".*

The influence of lost letters is also related to the question of stress and accent. The stress in Gaelic falls on the first syllable of the word no matter how long the word may be, eg *ath*arrachadh, "change"; apparent exceptions, such as **airson**, "for", which is stressed on the second syllable, are really two words – in this case **air son**, "on account (of)". Until fairly recently two accents were used, the grave (ˋ) and the acute (ˊ). These are placed above long vowels which have a stress. In such cases "a", "u" and "i" always had a grave accent, eg **fàs**, "grow", **cìr**, "comb", **ùr**, "new". A grave accent above "o" and "e" indicated the "open" sound of these vowels, ie like "o" and "e" in English "form" and "herd", eg **òr**, "gold", **cè**, "cream". An acute accent over "o" and "e" indicated the "closed" sound of these vowels, as in English "more" and "rein", e.g; **có?**, "who?", **dé?**, "what?". There is a growing tendency, however, to do away with the acute accent and to use only the grave instead, as recommended in the recent (1981) reform of Gaelic spelling.

The accent is useful in written Gaelic to distinguish words which would otherwise have the same spelling. Some common instances are:

aithne	knowledge	**àithne**	commandment
am	the	**àm**	time
ath	next	**àth**	ford (m), kiln (f)
bas	palm (of hand)	**bàs**	death
bata	a stick	**bàta**	boat

---

*Compare, in English, the words "adder" (originally "nadder" – Gaelic **nathair**, "snake") and "orange" (which also originally began with "n"). The converse, which also happens in Gaelic, is seen in words like "newt", originally "ewt".

bith existence	**bìth** gum, glue
brath spying	**bràth** judgement
caise short temper	**càise** cheese
caraid friend	**càraid** pair, couple
dail dale	**dàil** delay
de of	**dè**? what?
fad length	**fàd** a peat
faisg near	**fàisg** press, squeeze
feith wait	**fèith** sinew
gabhadh let (him etc) take	**gàbhadh** danger
gun without	**gùn** gown
sabaid fight	**Sàbaid** Sunday
samhach a handle	**sàmhach** quiet
sin that	**sìn** stretch

Of course the context usually makes it clear which word is meant.

In many Gaelic words the stressed long vowel with accent compensates for a consonant lost from Indo-European, as can be seen from the English cognate, eg **cìs**, "tax" (census)*, **mìos**, "month" (mensual). In fact, many long vowels and diphthongs are there to compensate for a lost consonant, eg **neul**, "cloud" (nebulous), **ceud**, "hundred" (century).

VOCABULARY

Gaelic	English	English Cognate
anam	soul	animate
bò	cow	bovine
borb	fierce	barbarian
ceart	right	certain
ceil	hide	conceal
èirich	rise	erect
fion	wine	vine

*Compare also English "excise".

marbh	dead	morbid
ràmh	oar	trireme
sabhal	barn	stable
sàl	sea	saline
sgillinn	penny	shilling (old Scots)
sgìre	district	shire
trang	busy	throng

6

Some Problems with Verbs

THE MAIN difficulties with the verb in Gaelic concern the verb "to be", the irregular verbs, and the verbal noun, each of which will now be considered.

Like some other languages (eg Italian and Spanish), Gaelic has two verbs "to be", usually referred to by their present tense forms **tha** and **is**. **Tha** ("am", "is", "are") is the commoner of the two; its past tense is **bha** ("was", "were"). The past tense of **is** is **bu**. The two verbs, however, are not directly interchangeable. **Is** is used when we wish to emphasise a particular word in a sentence, and this word follows the verb, eg **is mòr mo mhulad**, "great is my sorrow". **Tha**, on the other hand, simply makes a statement without any particular emphasis, eg **tha mi sgìth**, "I'm tired". In addition, **is** is used in certain idiomatic phrases, eg **is toigh leam**, "I like", **is aithne dhomh**, "I know". **Tha** should not be used in such instances.

Tha is in origin not really a verb of existence but rather indicates state, status or condition, not usually permanent. That is why, for instance, it cannot be used as it stands to indicate the state or occupation of a person, but must have some form of the preposition **ann**, "in", after it. Thus "I was a boy" is not **bha mi balach** but rather **bha mi 'nam bhalach**.

Tha, which is cognate with Italian "sta" and Spanish "esta", basically means "stand", although it is, of course, used as a verb "to be" in all three languages. Compare Italian "come sta?", "how are you?" with Gaelic **ciamar a tha thu?**

The verb "to be" is irregular in most languages and **tha** is no exception. Its question form is **a bheil?** and its negative **chan eil**. The same forms in the past tense are **an robh?** and **cha robh**. The reason for these different forms is simply that they are, in origin, different verbs. Thus, rather than saying that **bha** is the past tense of **tha** we should really say that **bha** is used as the past tense of **tha**, just as in English "was" is used as the past tense of "am". In Gaelic the verb is the first word in the sentence, so **tha** is probably the most common start to a Gaelic sentence, particularly since the language has no simple present tense, as English "I sing", but has to use the form with the verb "to be", "I am singing", **tha mi a' seinn**. **Tha** is also used as a single word sentence, meaning "yes". This is because Gaelic does not really have words for the simple "yes" and "no"; instead, the verb used in the question is repeated. The equivalent in English would be something like "are you busy?" – "I am". Thus to any question beginning "is?" or "are?" – using **a bheil?** – the answer in Gaelic is **tha** if we mean "yes" and **chan eil** if we mean "no". In addition **tha** is frequently heard as the equivalent of English "um", expressing hesitancy in speech.

The verbs "to be" are also used in Gaelic to get round the fact that the language has no verb "to have" in its simple form. Instead of saying "I have a dog" Gaelic uses a phrase corresponding to "there is a dog at me", **tha cù agam**. **Agam** is for **aig mi** (which is never used) just as in English "I'd" is for "I had" or "I would". All the personal pronouns have special forms when used with prepositions like **aig**, "at", **air**, "on", **do**, "to" etc, and many of these forms are more complex than mere contractions. Most grammar books give a full table of such forms.

Apart from the verb "to be" Gaelic has only ten irregular verbs and so compares favourably in this respect with other European languages. As in other languages, it is the most common verbs which are irregular, and so beginners meet them early. Thus **rach**, "go" has **chaidh**, "went" as its past tense. In other irregular verbs the different forms have arisen because of the use of prefixes and the alternating of the stress accent between the first and second syllable. Compare the English "swear" and "answer". The latter form is simply "swear" with the prefix "an-" (meaning "in return", "against") but we can see how placing the stress on the first syllable – "answer" – has affected the sound (and spelling) of the second syllable "-swer", so that it may not be immediately recognised as the verb "swear". Gaelic irregular verb forms have been arrived at in a similar way, but the alterations are even greater. Thus in early Gaelic "(he) gets" is **fo-gheibh** where **fo** is the prefix and **gheibh** the verb. The stress was on the second syllable **gheibh**, and as often happens, the unstressed prefix **fo** eventually dropped off. So today "gets", or rather "will get"* is simply **gheibh**.

Now to ask a question in Gaelic we put **am** or **an** in front of the verb, so "does (he) get?", or "will (he) get?" was originally **am fo-gheibh?** In this phrase the stress is again on the second element which this time is **fo**. So again the unstressed end part dropped off, leaving **am fo-gh?** which is, today, **am faigh?**, "will (he) get?"

Other irregular verb forms have evolved in similar circumstances. Grammar books give all the different forms.

Participles, or verbal nouns (so called because although verbs, they can be used as nouns, eg "there was much coming and going") are unusual in Gaelic in that there is no one single way of forming them. In English the participle/verbal noun always ends in -ing. In Gaelic there are more than ten

---

*Future forms can sometimes have a present tense feeling in Gaelic.

different endings and it is really a matter of learning them all individually. The reason for such variety is that Gaelic has made use of different suffixes in the language. We can see that the same thing happened in English, where nouns are formed with the use of various suffixes, eg

-ade with "block" gives "blockade"
-age with "bond" gives "bondage"
-ance with "annoy" gives "annoyance"
-er with "treasure" gives "treasurer"
-cy with "bankrupt" gives "bankruptcy"
-dom with "free" gives "freedom"

and so on. In Gaelic the main relevant suffixes are -(e)adh, -t, -ail or -eil, -t(a)inn, – sinn, -eachd, -aidh, -se, -(e)amh; the spelling rule determines the precise form. Most of the participles are formed with one of these suffixes attached to the root, which in Gaelic is the imperative. Thus whereas English has used suffixes to form nouns, Gaelic has used them to form verbal nouns.

The most common suffix is -(e)adh, eg a' bualadh, "striking", from buail, "strike". This is also the form used in Gaelic words taken from English, eg a' smocadh, "smoking", a' fònadh, "phoning". This form is also used in some dialects where "standard" Gaelic has a different form; thus a' dèanamh, "doing", has the form a' dèanadh in Islay and elsewhere. Such variation is not untypical; there is often more than one form of the same participle. So "saying", for example, may be a' cantainn or a' cantail, "throwing" may be a' tilgeil or a' tilgeadh.

There are also verbs where the participle/verbal noun has the same form as the root, ie there is no change, eg òl, "drink", ag òl, "drinking", ruith, "run", a' ruith, "running". Most grammar books and dictionaries give all the participle forms, since there is otherwise no way in which the learner can become familiar with them.

Infinitives (the English form "to open") are the same as the participles/verbal nouns, but with the first letter aspirated if possible. Thus **dùin**, "shut", **a' dùnadh**, "shutting, **a dhùnadh**, "to shut". If the verb begins with a vowel or "f", then **dh** (as in the past tense – see chapter 2) is placed before the verb, eg **innis**, "tell", **a dh'innse**, "to tell", **fosgail**, "open", **a dh'fhosgladh**, "to open".

VOCABULARY

Gaelic	English	English Cognate
adhradh	worship	adore
bòrd	table	board
broc	badger	brock
calman	dove	columbine, Columba
capall	mare	cavalry
clag	bell	clock
coinean	rabbit	coney
fìor	true	verily, verify
mil	honey	mellifluous
minig	often	many
salach	dirty	sallow
seac	wither	desiccate
sgadan	herring	shad
speur	heaven	sphere

7

Dialects

LIKE OTHER languages, Gaelic has its share of dialects. This can be a problem for learners. There is still really no "standard" Gaelic in the same way as there is "standard" English. Each area has its own form of Gaelic, which can, on occasions, provide difficulties for someone from another area. Such diversity, with its consequent enrichment of the language, is a welcome feature of a living tongue. Beginners in the language, however, need some sort of standard form to learn. In previous centuries a non-Gaelic speaker who wished to learn Gaelic could simply go to a particular area of the Highlands and Islands and learn the language there. He or she was greatly helped in this by the extensive monoglot nature of many areas. Today, teaching aids mean that anyone can learn the language without necessarily setting foot in a Gaelic-speaking area; indeed, the now universal bilingualism there can be quite an impediment.

Thus there is an advantage in using a "standard" form of Gaelic as far as possible and such a standard is gradually evolving. Education is also a factor, eg Gaelic as SCE subject. The broadcasting of Gaelic on radio and television has also helped, in that professional broadcasters are aware that they are speaking to all of the Gaidhealtachd – and beyond – and therefore tend to exclude extreme forms of dialect of their own particular area. But, it must be stressed, it is only the more extreme provincialisms which are avoided in such cases, and it is still clear from a broadcaster's speech where he or she comes from. For most native speakers, however – the man in the croft – "standard" Gaelic is at best a shadowy notion, and when speaking they will use the dialect of their own area.

The position is rather similar to Scots, where there is no agreed standard form. All this has much to do with the fact that Gaelic, always more widely spoken than written, has lacked the status of a national language. Now that Gaelic is being used more extensively in print, there is a further impetus towards a standard form. In the past, dictionaries, for instance, tended to contain provincialisms peculiar to the dialect of the author, sometimes without warning the reader that such was the case. It is only recently, too, that a wholly Gaelic dictionary has appeared; previously Gaelic dictionaries gave the meaning of each Gaelic word in English – ie dictionaries were Gaelic-English (and vice-versa) – which speaks volumes for the perceived status of the language and its speakers.

The issue of dialects has been simplified, within the present century, by the regrettable dying out of the language in certain areas. eg Perthshire, Strathspey, St Kilda, Kintyre and so on.

As one might expect, dialect differences belong to two main categories, a) individual words, and b) pronunciation. Some examples of a) are **gealbhan**, the Islay word for "fire" (**teine**); **dar**, mainland Inverness-shire for "when" (**nuair**); **Ceusda**, Barra word for "Easter" (**Càisg**); **àsan**, Uist form of "they" (**iadsan**); **bùrn**, Harris and Lewis word for "water" (**uisge**).

Some examples of b) are the sound "e" for "a" in Islay, so that **mac**, "son", sounds like **mec**; the Hebridean soft "r" sounding rather like English "th", so that **air a' mhuir**, "on the sea", sounds like **aith a' mhuith**; the apparent dropping of an initial "d" in Lewis, so that **an-dè**, "yesterday", sounds like **an yey**; final -**(e)amh**, as in **a' dèanamh**, "doing", pronounced "oo" (as in English "foot") in Uist; the Lewis habit of not sounding the "t" of the article placed before masculine nouns beginning with a vowel, so that **an t-eilean**, "the island" sounds like **an eilean**.

VOCABULARY

Gaelic	English	English Cognate
aimsir	time	measure
amhairc	look at	mark
buidhe	yellow	bay
bùrn	water	burn
can	say	chant
clann	children	clan (borrowed from Gaelic)
croch	hang	crucify
mion, meanbh	small	minor
sgrìobh	write	scribe
sìth	peace	sit (ie be inactive)
slaod	drag	slide

8

Time and Number

THE USE of time and number in Gaelic differs from that of English in one or two ways. One to ten in Gaelic (with some English cognates) is:

1   **aon**   (unit)

2   **dà**   (dual) Unlike English, it takes a singular form of the noun, aspirated, a relic of the dual case found in old Gaelic (and other European languages); so "two dogs" is **dà chù**.

3   **trì**   (triple)

4   **ceithir** (quatrain)

5   **còig** (quin: "n" missing in Gaelic – see chapter 5)

6   **sia**

7   **seachd** (septet; no original "p" in Gaelic)

8   **ochd** (octet)

9   **naoi** (nonary)

10   **deich** (decade)

Unlike English, Gaelic has no independent words for 11 and 12, but says instead "one ten", "two ten":

11   **aon deug**

12   **dà dheug**

13   **trì deug** Note that **deich** takes the form **deug** from 11 onwards, just as English "ten" changes to "teen".

"Twenty" is **fichead** (English "vigesimal", French "vingt").
Gaelic continues to use the traditional score system of
counting, so that 30 is "ten on twenty", 40 is "two twenties"
and so on. Thus:

30	**deich air fhichead**
40	**dà fhichead**
50	**dà fhichead 's a deich**
60	**trì fichead**
70	**trì fichead 's a deich**
80	**ceithir fichead** (compare French *quatre vingt*)
90	**ceithir fichead 's a deich**

A "hundred" is **ceud**; "fifty" is more often **leth-cheud** (**leth** =
half), or **caogad**, a "thousand" is **mìle** and a "million" is
millean.

In naming years, Gaelic speakers often prefer to use
English because of the rather cumbersome method involved
in Gaelic. Thus, for 1983 one must say in Gaelic something
corresponding to "nine hundred ten (ie nineteen hundred),
four twenties and three" – **naoi ceud deug, ceithir fichead
's a trì**, or sometimes "a thousand, nine hundred, four twenties
and three" – **mìle, naoi ceud, ceithir fichead 's a trì**. Most
Gaelic speakers therefore simply say "nineteen eighty-three".

In an attempt to avoid the complexities of the score
system a new decimal system has recently been introduced,
with terms based on the already existing **caogad**, "fifty". Thus:

30	**trìthead**
40	**ceathrad**
50	**caogad**
60	**seasgad**
70	**seachgad**
80	**ochdad**
90	**naochad**

These are rarely heard but are used in some children's books and school texts.

Like English, Gaelic has separate words for "first", "second" etc. The ending **-(e)amh** corresponds to English -th.

1st	**a' chiad**
2nd	**an dara**
	or **an dàrna**
3rd	**an treas**
4th	**an ceathramh**
5th	**an còigeamh**
6th	**an siathamh**
7th	**an seachdamh**
8th	**an t-ochdamh**
9th	**an naoidheamh**
10th	**an deicheamh**

Unlike English, however, Gaelic has a separate set of numerical forms from one to ten, used only of people. Thus "three persons" in Gaelic is **triùir**. The list is:

aonar	one person
dìthis	two persons
triùir	three persons
ceathrar	four persons
còignear	five persons
sianar	six persons
seachdnar	seven persons
ochdnar	eight persons
naoinear	nine persons
deichnear	ten persons

To tell the time in Gaelic we need to know, in addition to the numerals, the following words:

uair hour   **leth-uair** half hour
mionaid minute   **cairteal** quarter
gu to   **an dèidh** after

So, "twenty past ten" is **fichead mionaid an dèidh a deich**; "a quarter to eleven" is **cairteal gu aon uair deug**.

The days of the week, which start with the prefix **Di-**, signifying "day", are mainly named after Roman gods and Celtic fasts. (**aoine** = fast).

Monday	**Diluain** (lunar, cf. French *Lundi*)
Tuesday	**Dimàirt** (Mars, cf. French *Mardi*)
Wednesday	**Diciadain** (first fast day – **ciad aoine**)
Thursday	**Diardaoin** (between two fasts – **eadar dà aoine**)
Friday	**Dihaoine** (fast day – **aoine**)
Saturday	**Disatharna** (Saturn)
Sunday	**Didòmhnaich** (*dominus* – lord), or **Latha na Sàbaid** (Sabbath Day)

A "week" is **seachdain** (**seachd** = seven) and a "fortnight" is **cola-deug**, from **còig latha deug** – inclusive counting, as in many other European languages.

There are Gaelic names for the months of the year, given in all grammars, but they are seldom used by native speakers, for good historical reasons. In a sense the use of the names is artificial in that they do not refer to specific months but rather to certain periods and events of the year. For instance **Gearran**, "February" is the gelding time, which was not necessarily restricted to the four weeks of February. The Gaelic names are increasingly used, however, as exact equivalents of the English months; most grammar books give the complete list.

The seasons are **Earrach**, "Spring", **Samhradh**, "Summer", **Foghar**, "Autumn" and **Geamhradh**, "Winter".

Some other days which have Gaelic names are:

Bealltainn	May Day, Beltane
A' Bhliadhn' Ùr	New Year
A' Chàisg	Easter
An Nollaig	Xmas
Oidhche Challainn	Hogmanay
Oidhche Shamhna	Hallowe'en

VOCABULARY

Gaelic	English	English Cognate
àrd	high	arduous
bròg	shoe	brogue
buachaill	herdsman	bucolic
comann	society	community
creag	rock	crag
creid	believe	creed
cridhe	heart	cardiac
ionga	claw	unguis
muir	sea	mere, marine
stad	stop	station
stang	pool, ditch	stagnant
sùlair	gannet	solan goose

9

Place Names

PLACE NAMES in Gaelic are of three main types:

1. The Gaelic is much the same as the English, usually because the English form is simply an approximate rendering of the Gaelic sound, conforming to English spelling conventions. Thus **Tom an t-Sabhail** ("the hillock of the barn") is Tomintoul, **Bogha Mòr** ("big submerged sea rock") is Bowmore.

2. The Gaelic and English are translations of each other, and so one obviously needs some knowledge of Gaelic to understand this type. Some examples are:

An t-Àth Leathann	Broadford
An Eaglais Bhreac	Falkirk (speckled – Scots "faw" – church)
Bail' Ùr an t-Slèibh	Newtonmore (new town on the moor)
Ceann Loch Gilb	Lochgilphead

3. The Gaelic name is quite different from the English, usually older, and with a topographical or historical reference quite separate from that of the English name. The most common examples are:

Baile Bhòid	(the town of Bute) Rothesay
Baile Dhubhthaich	(the town of St Duthus) Tain
Am Blàr Dubh	(the dark field) Muir of Ord
Bun Ilidh	(the mouth of the River Ilidh) Helmsdale
A' Chananaich	(the canon, canonry) Fortrose
A' Chomraich	(the sanctuary) Applecross
Ceann Loch Chille Chiarain	
	(the head of the loch of St Kieran's church) Campbeltown
Cille Chuimein	(St Cumine's church) Fort Augustus
Cill Rìmhinn	(church of the king's hill) St Andrews
An Gearasdan	(the garrison) Fort William
Inbhir Pheofharain	(the mouth of the River Peffery) Dingwall
Dùn Eideann	(fort on the hill slope) Edinburgh
A' Mhanachainn	(the monastery) Beauly
(Port) Sgioba	(ship port) Port Charlotte

Also some counties:

Cataibh	(land of the wild-cat people) Sutherland
Gallaibh	(land of the foreigners) Caithness

The flexibility of place names in earlier times is well illustrated by the fact that Caithness and **Cataibh** have the same root, although today they refer to different modern counties.

It is significant that most names of this type are on the mainland, which reflects the penetration of the English language. In fact, most Gaelic speakers from the Hebrides generally use the English form of these mainland names; the main exceptions to this are **Dùn Eideann** and **An Gearasdan**.

In general, the commonest roots for Gaelic place names are:

inbhir	mouth of a river	eg Inverness
ceann	head	eg Kinlochleven
rubha	promontory	eg Rhu
creag	rock	eg Craignure
baile	township	eg Ballygrant
srath	valley	eg Strathpeffer
caol	strait	eg Kyle
druim	ridge	eg Drumnadrochit
cill	cell, church	eg Kilmun
dùn	fort	eg Dunblane
taigh	house	eg Tighnabruaich
achadh	field	eg Achiltibuie

In the Hebrides and North West Highlands many of the place names are of Scandinavian origin, reflecting the period of Viking rule there (beginning c. 800AD) The most common roots here are **stadhir**, "farm" (which generally appears as "sta"), hence Tolsta, Scarista, Lusta, etc; **setr**, or **sætr**, "dwelling", "sheiling" (which generally appears as "shader"), hence Grimshader, Drinishader, Uigshader, etc; and **bolstadhr**, "small farm" (which appears as **bost** in eg Lewis and as **bus** in Islay), hence Shawbost, Leurbost, Carbost, etc, and Kinnabus etc.

VOCABULARY

Gaelic	English	English Cognate
àireamh	number	rhyme
abhainn	river	Avon
balla	wall	bailey
coire	kettle, cauldron	corrie
còrd	agree	accord
cruinn	round	crown
cùl	back	cul de sac (French)

dearg	red	dark
fàsach	desert	vastness
leagh	melt	leak
lighiche	doctor	leech
maor	crown officer	mayor
meud	size	metre

10

Basics

IN THE 1930s Miss Elaine Swanson, director of the New York Language Research Institute, suggested that a basic vocabulary of no more than three hundred words was all a foreign tourist needed to "get along" in English. To prove this she confined herself to no more than three hundred words for three months; she also suggested that this basic list applied to any language, and translated it into French, German and Italian.

Here then is Miss Swanson's list of (rather less than) three hundred words, with their equivalents in Gaelic. In the case of Gaelic (and, indeed, in other languages) there are of course instances where there is no simple equivalent, eg for the English "yes" and "no"; again, one Gaelic word will sometimes do for two English words, eg "do" and "make" (both **dèan**), or "think" and "thought" (both **smaoinich**). Other difficulties are mentioned in footnotes as they occur.

There is usually, of course, more than one Gaelic word which comes to mind as a possible translation, and so the following equivalents are, to that extent, subjective.

Prepositions

at - **aig**
after - **an dèidh**
for – **airson**
from – **bho**
in – **ann**
on – **air**
to – **do**
with – **le**

Conjunctions

and – **agus**
but – **ach**
if – **ma**
or – **no**
so – **mar sin**
that – **gu**

Pronouns

I – **mi**
he – **e**
me – **mi**
my – **mo**
she – **i**
their – **an**
you – **thu** (s), **sibh** (pl)
your – **do** (s), **bhur** (pl)

Interjections

goodbye – **slàn le**
hello – **halò**
oh! – **o!**

Articles

the – **am, an, a', na, nan** or **nam***

---

* depending on gender, number and case

Nature
fire – **teine**
light – **solas**
sun – **grian**

Business
bank – **banca**
pound – **not**
penny – **sgillinn**
money – **airgead**
office – **oifis**
manager – **fear-riaghlaidh**
show – **sealladh**
size – **meud**
shop – **bùth**
trouble – **dragh**
way – **slighe**

Travel
boat – **bàta**
car – **càr**
country – **dùthaich**
hotel – **taigh-òsda**
left – **clì**
place – **àite**
right – **deas**
station – **stèisean**
street – **sràid**
ticket – **tiocaid**
town – **baile**
train – **trèana**

Objects
bag – **màileid**
book – **leabhar**
letter – **litir**
telephone – **fòn**
thing – **rud**

story – **sgeul**
word – **facal**
picture – **dealbh**
nothing – **neoni**

Days of the week
Monday – **Diluain**
Tuesday – **Dimàirt**
Wednesday – **Diciadain**
Thursday – **Diardaoin**
Friday – **Dihaoine**
Saturday – **Disatharna**
Sunday – **Didòmhnaich**

Modifiers
again – **a-rithist**
all – **uile**
any – **sam bith**
big – **mòr**
clean – **glan**
cold – **fuar**
dear (expensive) – **daor**
down – **sìos**
easy – **furasda**
every – **gach**
good – **math**
happy – **sona**
here – **an seo**
how? – **ciamar?**
little – **beag**
long – **fada**
many – **mòran**
more – **tuilleadh**
married – **pòsda**
much – **mòran**
new – **ùr**
nice – **gasda**

no – (make the verb negative)
not – **cha**
now – **an dràsda**
old – **sean**
other – **eile**
piece – **pìos**
ready – **deiseil**
right (correct) – **ceart**
same – **ceudna**
slow – **mall**
some – **cuid**
sorry – **duilich**
that – **sin**
there – **an sin**
this – **seo**
too (excessive) – **ro**
also – **cuideachd**
up – **suas**
warm – **blàth**
very – **glè**
well – **gu math**
what? – **dè?**
when? – **cuin?**
where? – **càite?**
who? – **cò?**
why? – **carson?**

Food

bread – **aran**
butter – **ìm**
sweets – **suiteis**
coffee – **cofaidh**
egg – **ugh**
fruit – **meas**
meat – **feòil**
milk – **bainne**
salt – **salainn**
sugar – **siùcar**

vegetables – **glasraich**
water – **uisge**

Time

day – **latha**
evening – **feasgar**
hour – **uair**
minute – **mionaid**
month – **mìos**
morning – **madainn**
night – **oidhche**
time – **ùine**
today – **an-diugh**
tonight – **a-nochd**
tomorrow – **a-màireach**
week – **seachdain**
yesterday – **an-dè**

House

bath – **bath** *
floor – **làr**
house – **taigh**
key – **iuchair**
room – **seòmar**
table – **bòrd**

People

boy – **balach**
brother – **bràthair**
doctor – **dotair**
father – **athair**
friend – **caraid**
girl – **caileag**
man – **duine**
men – **daoine**
miss – **maighdeann**
mother – **màthair**

*Most Gaelic speakers simply use the English word

Mr – **maighstir**
Mrs – **bean-phòsda**
name – **ainm**
one – **aon**
policeman – **poileas**
sister – **piuthar**
woman – **boireannach**
women – **boireannaich**

Clothes

cloth – **clò**
clothes – **aodach**
coat – **còta**
dress – **dreasa**
hat – **ad**
shoes – **brògan**
stockings – **stocainnean**
trousers – **briogais**

Colour

black – **dubh**
blue – **gorm**
green – **uaine**
red – **dearg**
white – **geal**

Verbs

to – *
will – **-(a)idh**
won't – **cha**
ask – **faighnich**
be – **bi**
am – **tha**
are – **tha**
is – **tha**
was – **bha**
were – **bha**

* For the infinitive see chapter 6

can – **is urrainn**
can't – **chan urrainn**
could – **b'urrainn**
come – **thig**
came – **thàinig**
do – **dèan**
did – **rinn**
does – **tha (e) a' dèanamh**
don't (imperative) – **na**
eat – **ith**
ate – **dh'ith**
excuse – **gabh leisgeul**
get – **faigh**
got – **fhuair**
give – **thoir**
go – **rach**
went – **chaidh**
have – **tha aig**
has – **tha aig**
had – **bha aig**
have to – **feumaidh**
help – **cuidich**
know – **tha fios aig**
knew – **bha fios aig**
learn – **ionnsaich**
like – **is toigh le**
make – **dèan**
made – **rinn**
must – **feumaidh**
please – **toilich**
put – **cuir**
gain – **buannaich**
read – **leugh**
say – **abair**
said – **thubhairt**
see – **faic**
saw – **chunnaic**
sent – **chuir**

sit – **suidh**
sat – **shuidh**
sleep – **caidil**
slept – **chaidil**
smoke – **smoc**
start (begin) – **tòisich**
stop – **stad**
take – **gabh**
took – **ghabh**
thank – **thoir taing**
think – **smaoinich**
thought – **smaoinich**
understand – **tuig**
understood – **thuig**
use – **cuir gu feum**
want – **iarr**
work – **obraich**
write – **sgrìobh**
wrote – **sgrìobh**

VOCABULARY

Gaelic	English	English Cognate
amadan	fool	un-minded
balg	bag	bulge
bràghad	neck,throat	bronchial
bruich	boil, cook	brew, broth
caraid	friend	charity
connadh	fuel	candle
crùb	crouch	creep
cuileag	a fly	culex, culiciform
dàil	delay	dwell
duilich	sorry	dolour
fios	knowledge	vision
leugh	read	legible
màl	rent,payment	blackmail
meall	deceive	maltreat, malice
miann	desire	mean